PUBLISHED BY
SWAMI SIDDHESWARANANDA
PRESIDENT
SRI RAMAKRISHNA ASRAMA
MYSORE

TO

HIS HIGHNESS

SRI KRISHNARAJA WODEYAR BAHADUR IV,

G.C.S.I., G.B.E.

MAHARAJA OF MYSORE

IN HIGH ADMIRATION

OF HIS GREAT DEVOTION TO VEDANTIC TRUTH

FOREWORD

It is a matter of general knowledge that a Hindu not infrequently exclaims, when he finds anything supremely difficult to achieve or understand, " It is like *Brahmavidyā* ! " This *Brahmavidyā* or knowledge of Brahman, the attainment of which is thought to be so hard, is acquired only gradually, the steps being those of religion, theology including scholasticism, mysticism and philosophy including science. All these are comprehended by the term Vedānta. Men's knowledge of science having been in its infancy, in the past, it was treated not as a separate subject but as a part of philosophy, which is a *rational* enquiry regarding all that is known to exist. Though philosophy or *Vichāra* comes last, yet it is not introduced abruptly at the very end. Every one, each to the extent to which one's *Buddhi* or reasoning power admits, is by nature free to exercise this faculty, at whatever stage one may be. And as a consequence even the preliminary stages are mistaken by the ignorant for philosophy though the last alone is specifically so called, because it is then that one is able to devote oneself exclusively to a pursuit of the highest or the most comprehensive Truth, by means of *Buddhi* (reason).

In the past, *rigorous* Yogic (mystic) discipline, which was not an end in itself, helped to so clarify the mind as to enable it to reason most correctly. But such discipline is almost impossible under present conditions. The modern mental outlook is pre-eminently scientific owing to the great progress that science has made. And the best method of freeing the mind from its inaccurate ways of thinking is to imbue it as fully as possible with the scientific spirit. It is therefore only one who possesses a clear knowledge of its methods and results *i.e.*, who is able to make reason (*Buddhi*) the highest means of enquiry that would be fit to enter upon the study of Vedantic *philosophy*.

For, as Vedanta itself admits its highest Truth (Ātman or Brahman) cannot be reached by any path other than that of *Buddhi* (reason) and unless the *Buddhi* is sharper than the 'Edge of a razor' (*Kath. Up.*, III, 12 and III, 14), which is also characterized as *Mahādhi* or *Mahābuddhi* (great or supreme reason) elsewhere (*Māndukya Kārikā*, IV, 89). The Gītā also supports it in several places (*vide* X, 10 and VI, 21). Further, where *Manas* and *Chitta* are used in the sense of *Buddhi* in Vedāntic literature, they are declared to be the highest means of attaining such knowledge (*Brih. Up.*, IV, 4, 19, *Mund. Up.*, III, 1, 9, and *Kath. Up.*, IV, 11). Contrariwise, it is expressly stated that neither religion, theology nor mystic practice is in itself of value in the absence of

Buddhi (*vide Kath. Up.*, III, 23 and *Mund.*, III, 1, 8). The aim of every one should be to reach this supreme level of *Buddhi*, by continued enquiry, though one may feel satisfied with the religion, theology or mysticism in which one believes. Some have not the patience to pursue it to the end. Therefore, the highest stage to which most men attain is only the theological (based on authority) or the mystic (based on intuition), and not the rational. How then, it may be asked, is such high order of *Buddhi* to be reached and how so much of patience to be commanded? The Vedānta says:

"None who has not turned away from bad conduct, whose senses are not under control, whose mind is not collected, or whose mind is not at rest, can attain this Ātman by means of intelligence."—(*Kath. Up.*, II, 24.)

"This Ātman is obtainable by love of *truth*, by *austerity*, by *correct knowledge*, by one's life of *chastity* (*Brahmacharya*) constantly practised."—(*Mund. Up.* III, 1, 4.)

In a word, purity of life, comprehending thought, word, and deed, is the foremost requisite for sharpening the *Buddhi*.

Recognizing, therefore, the difficulty of the nature of the study of Vedānta *as a whole*, some of the leading authorities on it have written a number of manuals of introduction. Though all these treatises cover the same ground, refer to the same topics of importance, and point to the same goal, yet they differ from each other in their *approach* to the subject. Since these manuals are meant to lead those in the lower stages to rational (*Buddhi*), *i.e.*, philosophic enquiry (*Vichāra*), they largely cover the preliminary, *i.e.*, the religious, theological and mystic stages of Vedānta, indicating directly or indirectly the way to the final, *i.e.*, the rational means of attaining the goal. All of them rely on the authority of Vedic Revelation and mystic or Yogic ecstasy of *Samādhi*. But the *philosophy*, which rises still higher into realms of pure Reason, is evidently reserved for more advanced enquiry.

The importance of *Dṛg-Dṛśya Vivēka* as an aid to the study of Vedānta has been well pointed out by the learned Swami Nikhilanandaji in his introduction to this translation. The central theme of this work is that Brahman is realized through mystic or Yogic *Samādhi* (Concentration). *After* this state is attained, one can see Brahman wherever one turns one's eyes.

" Déhābhimāne galite vijnāte paramātmani
Yatra yatra mano yāti tatra tatra Samādhayaha "

" With the disappearance of the attachment to the body and with the realization of the Supreme Self, to whatever object the mind is directed one experiences *Samādhi*."

Problems such for instance as how to make sure that after we attain *Samādhi* whatever we see is the Supreme Being or Brahman and not anything else, are matters beyond the scope of this small treatise.

Dṛg-Dṛśya Vivēka being very short, it necessarily compresses much information into a small space. Detailed explanations are indispensable. Swami Nikhilanandaji has spared no pains to make not only the English rendering accurate, but also the notes exhaustive and scholarly, which will be found to be of immense help to those who wish to proceed to a higher study of Vedāntic philosophy.

The Swami's great literary merits are already so well and so widely known that this work of his needs little introduction from laymen like me. It is a time-honoured belief, a belief as old as the oldest Upanishads, that Vedāntic Truth is best taught by those that live it, but not by those that merely talk it. Bhagavan Sri Ramakrishna Paramahamsa, the 'Real Mahatma' of the late Prof. Max Müller, was one such rare and great teacher. And the Vedāntic works that are published by the revered Order of Sannyasins founded by such a Guru have so great a spiritual charm that they make these works most welcome to all earnest seekers after Truth.

Mysore. V. SUBRAHMANYA IYER.

INTRODUCTION

Dṛg-Dṛśya Vivēka, as the name indicates, is an inquiry into the distinction of the 'Seer' (*Dṛg*) and the 'Seen' (*Dṛśya*)—an inquiry which is of the utmost importance for the understanding of the higher Vedānta Philosophy. The other name by which this treatise is known is *Vākya Suddhā* ascribed to Sankarāchārya, which is also the name of a commentary on it. *Dṛg-Dṛśya Viveka* has been acknowledged as a *Prakarana* treatise of the Vedānta Philosophy, *i.e.*, a book which, though confined to a particular aspect of the subject-matter, explains its chief purpose, *viz.*, the identification of Jiva and Brahman, by following a particular line of argument. The special feature of this book is its detailed description of the various kinds of Samādhi (Concentration), the importance of which is always acknowledged by the students of Vedānta. It has also given three theories, necessarily empirical in character, regarding the conception of Jiva (embodied being).

This small book of forty-six Ślokas, is an excellent *vade mecum* for the study of higher Vedānta. Sixteen of the Ślokas from *Dṛg-Dṛśya Vivēka*, from 13 to 31 with the exception of 14, 21 and 28, are found in a minor

Upanishad, called the *Saraswati Rahasyopanishad.* It does not seem probable that the author of *Dṛg-Dṛśya Vivēka* wrote a treatise of forty-six stanzas borrowing sixteen from another book. Neither of the two commentators has mentioned these sixteen Ślokas as quotation from the Upanishad in question. Therefore it seems to us that the author of the Upanishad has borrowed these Ślokas from *Dṛg-Dṛśya Vivēka*, which, if true, would indicate the importance of the book.

Three names are generally associated with the authorship of the book. Brahmānanda Bhārati, one of the commentators, acknowledges Bhārati Tirtha as its author. In some manuscripts it is found that Ānanda Jnāna, another commentator, salutes in the colophon Sankarāchārya as its author. Nischaladāsa, in his *Vritti Prabhākara*, ascribes the book to Vidyāranya, the celebrated author of *Panchadaśi.* We are led to think that the book was written by Bhārati Tirtha. Brahmānanda Bhārati probably wrote, as some authorities hold, a commentary called *Vākya Suddhā.* Bhārati Tirtha, the teacher of Vidyāranya, was a Jagad Guru of the Sringeri Math founded by Sankarāchārya. The old records of the Math state that he was the head of the Math from 1328 to 1380 A.D. An inscription dated 1340 A.D. states that Harihara I, the ruler of Vijayanagar, and his brothers made grants of land to Bhārati Tirtha for the maintenance of the Sringeri

Math. Probably Bhārati Tirtha was also known as Ānanda Bhārati Tirtha. Bhārati Tirtha is associated with the authorship of *Dṛg-Dṛśya Vivēka*, *Vaiyāsikanyāyamālā* and a portion of *Panchadaśi*. *Vaiyāsikanyāyamālā* is of great help to the student in understanding the commentary of Sankarāchārya on the *Brahma-sūtra*.

There are two commentaries extant of *Dṛg-Dṛśya Vivēka*. One is by Brahmānanda Bhārati and the other by Ānanda Jnāna or Ānandagiri. The book has been translated into several languages. The Bengali translation has been admirably done by Babu Durgācharan Chattopādhyāya, the erudite Sanskrit scholar of Benares, to whom we are obliged for much of the information given in this introduction.

Dṛg-Dṛśya Vivēka, in dealing with certain aspects of the subject-matter, follows a method which may be called rational in that it attempts to discuss by employing a method which is known in logic as the method of Agreement and Disagreement or the method of *Anvaya Vyatireka* of the Indian Nyāya system. The book, it is hoped, will be of considerable help to those who wish to pursue the higher study of Vedānta Philosophy.

For the facility of understanding by the average student, we have given, besides the meaning of the words of the text and its running translation, extensive notes mainly collected from the two commentaries mentioned above. The Telugu, Malayālam, English, Sanskrit and Bengali editions of the book, which we have consulted while translating the treatise, have not always the same reading. We have not followed *in toto* any of these editions. But our reading will be supported by one or the other of the books we have consulted.

We wish to take this opportunity to express our sense of deep gratitude to H. H. Sri Krishnaraja Wodeyar IV, Maharaja of Mysore, for so kindly permitting us to associate this book with his name. Sri Ramakrishna Āsrama at Mysore owes its present position of usefulness to his sympathy and generosity. It is well known that His Highness' noble father encouraged Swāmi Vivekānanda to proceed to the Parliament of Religions held in Chicago, an event which has raised India in the estimation of the whole of the civilized world. The Maharaja's deep knowledge of philosophy, Eastern and Western, besides his remarkable acquaintance with modern science has made him one of the most cultured and respected of India's rulers.

THE AUTHOR.

॥ ओं परमात्मने नमः ॥

॥ दृग्दृश्य विवेकः ॥

(DRG-DRŚYA VIVĒKA)

रूपं दृश्यं लोचनं दृक् तद्दृश्यं दृक्तु मानसं ।
दृश्याधीवृत्तयस्साक्षी दृगेव न तु दृश्यते ॥ १ ॥

रूपं form दृश्यं (is) perceived लोचनं eye दृक् (is) perceiver तत् that दृश्यं (is) perceived मानसं mind दृक् (is) perceiver धीवृत्तयः mind's modifications दृश्याः (are) perceived साक्षी Witness दृक् एव (is) verily the perceiver तु but न (it) is not दृश्यते perceived.

1. The form[1] is perceived and the eye[2] is its perceiver.[3] It (eye) is perceived and the mind[4] is its perceiver. The mind with[5] its modifications is perceived and the Witness (the Self) is verily the perceiver.[6] But It[7] (the Witness) is not perceived (by any other).

The direct and immediate knowledge of Ātman or Self is the means to the attainment of Liberation. The understanding of the meaning of the great Vedic statement "That thou art" (तत्त्वमसि) enables one to realise the goal of life. The meaning of "That thou art" is correctly grasped by understanding the sense of the words contained in the statement. The first five slokas in the treatise explain the significance of 'Thou'.

[1] *Form*—The word implies all objects of sense perception.

[2] *Eye*—It stands for all the organs of perception such as nose, ears etc.

[3] *Perceiver*—The eye is perceiver only in a relative sense because it is itself perceived by the mind.

[4] *Mind*—The sense organs, unless the mind is attached to them, cannot perceive their objects. In a state of deep sleep the sense organs do not perceive anything because the mind, at that time, ceases to function.

[5] *With etc.*—This includes Buddhi, Chitta, and Ahamkāra.

[6] *Perceiver*—The mind is controlled by the conscious Self. Comp. "अन्यत्रमना अभूवं नादर्शं "(बृ. उ. १-५-३) "My mind was elsewhere; I did not see."

[7] *It*—The Ātman or the innermost Self is the ultimate perceiver. If a perceiver of the Ātman is sought, the enquiry will end in what is known as a *regressus ad infinitum*. All entities from the gross objects to the mind are products of Avidyā which itself is insentient (जड). Hence they also partake of the nature of insentiency. Therefore they are objects. The subjective character of some of these is only relative. But the Self is the ultimate Seer because no other seer is known to exist. The knowledge of the Knower is never absent.

The subject matter of the first sloka is explained in detail in the following:—

II

नीलपीतस्थूलसूक्ष्महृस्वदीर्घादि भेदतः ।
नानाविधानि रूपाणि पश्येल्लोचनमेकधा ॥ २ ॥

नीलपीतस्थूलसूक्ष्महृस्वदीर्घादि भेदतः on account of such distinctions as blue, yellow, gross, subtle, short, long etc. नानाविधानि various रूपाणि forms लोचनं the eye एकधा as one पश्येत् perceives.

2. The forms (objects of perception) appear as various on account of such distinctions as blue, yellow, gross, subtle, short, long etc. The eye, on the other hand, sees them, itself remaining one and the same.

The forms etc. are objects of perception which are varying. That which is constant and changeless is the perceiver. The different objects appear, no doubt, as distinct from one another. But they are perceived with their changes, because the eye, as perceiver, is a unity. They all belong to one category, namely, दृश्य or the seen. With reference to the objects, the eye is the perceiver.

The one characteristic of the objects is their changeability. Change is possible only in things which are imagined with reference to a substratum, as is the case with the snake, stick, water-line, garland etc., falsely imagined in a rope. These ideas are subject to change. The characteristic of the Seer is unchangeability. The objects change but their perceiver is constant. The appearances, like the snake etc., change but the rope is constant.

III

The eye, on account of its changeable nature, is an object and its perceiver is the mind.

आन्ध्यमान्द्यपटुत्वेषु नेत्रधर्मेषु चैकधा ।
संकल्पयेन्मनः श्रोत्रत्वगादौ योज्यतामिदम् ॥ ३ ॥

आन्ध्यमान्द्यपटुत्वेषु blindness, dullness and sharpness, नेत्रधर्मेषु characteristics of the eye मनः mind एकधा as a unity संकल्पयेत् cognizes इदं this श्रोत्रत्वगादौ to ears, skin, etc., च also योज्यतां applies.

3. Such characteristics of the eye as blindness, sharpness or dullness, the mind is able to cognize because it is a unity. This also applies to (whatever is perceived through) the ear, skin etc.

Though the eye is the perceiver in respect of the various forms, yet it becomes the object of perception in its relation to the mind. The eye is subject to changes which are perceived by the mind ; for it is the mind that thinks 'I am blind' etc. The mind knows the changes because it is a unity. This applies to the other sense-organs as well. Though the nose, the skin, the tongue etc. are respectively perceivers with reference to their several objects, yet they themselves are perceived by the mind. Hence, the mind is perceiver and the sense-organs are objects of perception.

IV

Mind, also like other sense-organs, is an object perceived by another. This is indicated in the following sloka :—

कामः संकल्पसंदेहौ श्रद्धाश्रद्धे धृतीतरे ।
ह्रीर्धीर्भीरित्येवमादीन् भासयत्येकधा चितिः ॥ ४ ॥

चितिः Consciousness कामः desire संकल्पसंदेहौ determination and doubt श्रद्धाश्रद्धे faith and want of faith धृतीतरे steadiness and its opposite ह्रीः modesty धीः understanding भीः fear इत्येवमादीन् and such others एकधा unified भासयेत् illumines.

4. Consciousness illumines (such other mental states as) desire[1], determination[2] and doubt, belief[3] and non-belief, constancy[4] and its opposite, modesty, understanding, fear and others,[5] because it (Consciousness) is a unity.

[1] *Desire*—Desire for the satisfaction of sensual pleasure.

[2] *Determination*—Determining the nature of objects directly perceived by a sense-organ.

[3] *Faith*—Faith in the result of Karma and the existence of God.

[4] *Steadiness*—The mental power which sustains a man even while he is physically or otherwise tired.

[5] *Others etc.*—Other states or functions of the mind are enumerated in the *Aitareya Upanishad* (3-2).

The list of the states or functions of the mind has been adopted from *Bṛhadāraṇyaka Upanishad* (1-5-3).

V

That the mind undergoes all these changes is known to all. Because of its changeable nature, the mind is an object of perception and Consciousness is the perceiver. This is because all these changes are perceived by Consciousness. Consciousness perceives all these states because it is a unity. These states, though distinct in nature, become unified in Consciousness or Self.

नोदेति नास्तमेत्येषा न वृद्धिं याति न क्षयम् ।
स्वयं विभात्यथान्यानि भासयेत्साधनं विना ॥ ५ ॥

एषा This (Consciousness) न उदेति does not rise न अस्तम् एति does not set वृद्धिं increase न याति does not undergo क्षयं decay न (याति) does not undergo स्वयं of itself विभाति shines अथ on the other hand विना without साधनं aid (of other means) अन्यानि other objects भासयेत् illumines.

5. This Consciousness[1] does neither rise[2] nor set[3]. It does[4] not increase; nor does it suffer decay. Being self-luminous, it illumines everything[5] else without any other aid.

[1] *Consciousness*—It is the eternal Witness of all internal changes.

[2] *Neither rise*—'Rising' means birth, *i.e.*, coming into existence of an entity previously non-existent. This cannot be predicated of Consciousness as it is the Witness of even previous non-existence. Otherwise no one will be aware of such non-existence. All entities from the empirical ego to the gross object perceived have a previous non-existing state, because their appearance and disappearance are cognized by consciousness.

[3] *Set*—' Setting ' means disappearance of an existing entity, *i.e.*, its becoming non-existent again This state, though possible for relative entities, cannot be predicated of Consciousness. No disappearance or destruction can be cognized without a conscious Witness.

[4] *Does not etc.*—Every perceived entity of the empirical world possesses six characteristics, *viz.*, birth (जन्म), existence (अस्तित्व), growth (वृद्धि), change (विपरिणाम), decay (अपक्षय) and destruction (नाश). But Consciousness has none of the characteristics of a perceived entity. By negating birth and decay, the four other characteristics are also negated in Consciousness. Growth and decay are only possible for those entities which have parts. But Consciousness is without parts.

[5] *Everything else*—All perceived entities. Comp. "तमेव भान्तं अनुभाति सर्वं तस्य भासा सर्वमिदं विभाति " "It shining, all else shines" (*Katha Upanishad* 5-15). It is because there is nothing else to illumine the Ātman : it is self-luminous.

VI

चिच्छायावेशतो बुद्धौ भानं धीस्तु द्विधा स्थिता ।
एकाहंकृतिरन्या स्यादंतःकरणरूपिणी ॥ ६ ॥

बुद्धौ in the Buddhi (intelligence) चिच्छाया reflection of Consciousness आवेशतः on account of entering भानं appearance (of specific knowledge) भवति happens धीः intelligence (understanding) तु and द्विधा of two kinds स्थिता is एका one अहंकृतिः egoity स्यात् is अन्या other अंतःकरणरूपिणी of the nature of mind (mental faculties).

6. Buddhi appears to possess luminosity[1] on account of the reflection of Consciousness in it. Intelligence (Buddhi)[2] is of two kinds[3]. One is designated egoity (अहंकृतिः), the other as mind (अन्तःकरणं).

[1] *Luminosity*—The Conscious Self (चिदात्मा), though self-luminous, has no manifestation, because from the absolute standpoint there is no other object which can be manifested by Consciousness. But on account of the superimposition of ignorance (अविद्या) a modification appears known as mind (अंतःकरणं) which though insentient (जड) (being the product of अविद्या) appears as conscious on account of the association of consciousness or Ātman with it. The Ātman appears as Buddhi when associated with Antahkarana. The Buddhi, on account of its association with Consciousness, appears to be endowed with agency, will etc.

[2] *Buddhi*—Buddhi or Dhīh or intelligence is the internal organ which is subject to various modifications. The modification which makes and endows it with agency etc., is known as Ahamkṛti or Ahamkāra or egoism. Another modification is known as memory consisting of various faculties by means of which external objects are perceived. The Buddhi, by itself, is insentient (जड). But its appearance as subject, object and the means of perception is possible on account of the reflection of Consciousness (चित्) in it. This reflection endows Buddhi with the power of perceiving objects.

[3] *Two kinds*—When Consciousness is reflected in Buddhi it undergoes two main modifications. These are the ego and the mind. The ego implies a subject (अहंकार) as well as its mind (अंतःकरणं). The inner organ, according to its different functions, is known

as volition and doubt (मनस्), determining faculty (बुद्धि) and the faculty of memory (चित्त).

VII

According to the first sloka, the eye and the mind have been described as seers with respect to their several objects of perception. But they are insentient. Therefore a doubt arises as to their power of cognition. This doubt is solved by the following sloka which says that though the mind etc. are insentient, yet on account of the reflection of Consciousness (चित्) in them, they appear to be conscious. Hence knowledge of objects is possible for them.

छायाहंकारयोरैक्यं तप्तायःपिंडवन्मतं ।
तदहंकारतादात्म्याद्देहश्चेतनतामगात् ॥ ७ ॥

छायाहंकारयोः of the reflection and egoism ऐक्यं identity तप्त अयःपिंडवत् is like the identity of fire and the heated iron ball मतम् opinion (of the wise) तत् that अहंकार egoism तादात्म्यात् owing to the identification देहः body चेतनतां consciousness अगात् has attained.

7. In the opinion of the wise, the identity of the reflection (of Consciousness) and of ego[1] is like the identity[2] of the fire and the (heated) iron ball. The body[3] having been identified with the ego (which has already identified itself with the reflection of Consciousness) passes for a conscious[4] entity.

[1] *Ego*—It is associated with the notion of subject.

[2] *Identity*—In the case of a red-hot iron ball, fire and iron appear to be identified with each other. Similarly the reflection of Consciousness, coming in contact with ego, becomes completely identified with it and they cannot be separated from each other. This reflection of Consciousness which identifies itself with the insentient Ahamkāra is what is known as Jīva or embodied being.

[3] *Body*—Which is otherwise inert and insentient.

[4] *Conscious entity*—That is, movement etc. are ascribed to the body on account of this identification. Consciousness (साक्षीचैतन्य) imparts the appearance of sentiency to all objects from egoism to the gross body, because it is the innermost essence of all The body includes the places where the sense-organs are located. Therefore there is no separate identification with the sense-organ.

VIII

Now is described the nature of the identification of Ahamkāra with different entities :—

अहंकारस्य तादात्म्यं चिच्छायादेहसाक्षिभिः ।
सहजं कर्मजं भ्रान्तिजन्यं च त्रिविधं क्रमात् ॥ ८ ॥

अहंकारस्य of the ego तादात्म्यं identification चिच्छाया देहसाक्षिभिः with the reflection of Consciousness, body and Witness क्रमात् respectively सहजं natural कर्मजं due to past Karma भ्रांतिजन्यं च and due to ignorance त्रिविधं of three kinds (भवति is).

8. The identification of the ego[1] with the reflection of Consciousness, the body and the

Witness are of three kinds, namely, natural,[2] due to (past) Karma,[3] and due to ignorance,[4] respectively.

[1] *Ego*—See *ante.* sloka 6.

[2] *Natural*—The moment the reflection of Consciousness and the ego (Ahamkāra) come into existence, they become identified with each other. The ego manifests itself under the influence of this reflection. Therefore this identification is called natural or innate. The experience resulting from this identification is, "I know" (अहं जानामि).

[3] *Karma*—The ego identifies itself with a particular body according to its past acts, virtuous or otherwise. Birth in a particular body is always determined by Karma. The experience resulting from this identification is, "I am man" (अहं मनुष्यः).

[4] *Ignorance.*—Ignorance of the real nature of Consciousness is called here भ्रांति (delusion) which is without beginning and cannot be described as 'Real' or 'Unreal'. This identification of the Ahamkāra (ego) with the Witness (साक्षीचैतन्य) is based only upon ignorance (भ्रांति). This identification can be removed only by knowing the real nature of Consciousness. The experience resulting from this identification is, "I am or exist" (अहमस्मि).

IX

How the different identifications of the Ahamkāra come to an end is thus described :—

संबंधिनोस्सतोर्नास्ति निवृत्तिस्सहजस्य तु ।
कर्मक्षयात् प्रबोधाच्च निवर्तेते क्रमादुभे ॥ ९ ॥

संबन्धिनोः of the mutually related (ego and the reflection of Consciousness) सतोः of those that are taken to be real सहजस्य natural (तादात्म्यस्य of the identification) तु certainly निवृत्तिः annihilation नास्ति is not possible उभे the other two कर्मक्षयात् with the wearing away of the (result of) Karma प्रबोधाच्च and enlightenment क्रमात् respectively निवर्तेते disappear.

9. The mutual identification of the ego and the reflection of Consciousness, which[1] is natural, does[2] not cease so long as they are taken to be real. The other[3] two identifications disappear after the wearing[4] out of the result of Karma and the attainment[5] of the knowledge of the highest Reality respectively.

[1] *Which etc.*—The moment the ego (अहंकार) and the reflection of Consciousness come into existence they identify themselves with each other.

[2] *Does not etc.*—That is, they can never separate themselves from each other so long as they are taken to be real. It is like the reflection of the sun in the water in a pot. The reflection can never separate itself from the water. The reflection disappears only when the water pot ceases to be.

[3] *Other two.*—The identifications of the ego with the body and the Witness (साक्षी).

[4] *Wearing out etc.*—The identification of the ego with the body is due to the past Karma whose effect is seen in this body that lasts till the Karma continues to produce its effects. But when the body comes to an end owing to the complete wearing out of the effects of Karma its identification with the ego automatically

ceases. This phenomenon is also observed at the time of swoon and deep sleep when the effects of Karma are temporarily suspended.

[5] *Attainment etc.*—The identification of the ego with the Consciousness (साक्षीचैतन्य) is due to error (भ्रांति) which is destroyed only by the attainment of Knowledge. Knowledge (ज्ञानं) destroys ignorance (अज्ञानं) and its effects. Ahamkāra or the ego is the effect of ignorance. Therefore it is also destroyed by Knowledge. Hence Ahamkāra can no longer identify itself with the Witness after enlightenment, when it disappears in Brahman.

The three kinds of identification described above disappear simultaneously when the Jīva realizes itself as Brahman.

X

Now is described the world-bound nature of the Ātman as well as its associations with the three states, which are possible only when the ego identifies itself with the body :—

अहंकारलये सुप्तौ भवेद्देहोऽप्यचेतनः ।
अहंकार विकासार्धस्स्वप्नस्सर्वस्तु जागरः ॥ १० ॥

सुप्तौ in deep sleep अहंकारलये when (the thought of) ego disappears देहः the body अपि also अचेतनः unconscious भवेत् becomes अहंकार-विकासार्धः the half manifestation of the ego स्वप्नः dream (भवति is) तु but सर्वः full (manifestation) जागरः waking state (भवति is).

10. In the state of deep sleep, when (the thought of) ego disappears[1] the body also becomes unconscious. The state in which there is the half manifestation of the ego is called the dream state[2] and the full[3] manifestation of the ego is the state of waking.

[1] *Disappears*—The ego merges itself in the causal ignorance which is characterised by the non-apprehension of empirical objects. This state in which there is no perception of duality is called the state of deep sleep. The ego in this state does not identify itself with the body. The result of past Karma, then, is not noticed. Therefore we become unconscious of our body in that state. Comp. "अंधःसन्ननंधो भवति विद्धः-सन्नविद्धो भवति उपतापी सन्ननुपतापी भवति" (छां. उ. ८-४-२). "(Therefore he who has crossed that bank) if blind, ceases to be blind ; if wounded, ceases to be wounded : if afflicted, ceases to be afflicted."

[2] *Dream state*—In the dream state the ego does not perceive any object external to itself. The seer, the objects seen and the act of seeing which constitute the dream experiences are only the mental modifications of the ego. Compare—

"न तत्र रथा न रथयोगा न पंथानो भवंति" (बृ. उ. ४-३-१०)

"There are no (real) chariots in that state, no horses, no roads (but he himself creates chariots, horses and roads)." The dream experiences, though they appear during the dream state as outside the body of the seer, are known to be only modifications of the mind from the standpoint of the waking state. Therefore from the waking standpoint the dream state is only a partial manifestation of the ego.

[3] *Full manifestation*—In the waking state the ego experiences the gross external objects by means of its

internal organs. The ego and the non-ego which constitute the entire world of experience are both cognized in the waking state. In dream it is the mind alone of the sleeper which appears both as the ego and the non-ego. Therefore the full manifestation of the experience covering both ego and non-ego is seen only in the waking condition.

XI

How the experiences of the waking and dream states are but the modifications of mind is described now:—

अंतःकरणवृत्तिश्च चितिच्छायैक्यमागता ।
वासनाः कल्पयेत्स्वप्नेबोधेऽक्षैर्विषयान्बहिः ॥ ११ ॥

अन्तःकरणवृत्तिश्च the inner organ that is nothing but a modification (वृत्तिः) चितिच्छायैक्यं identity with the reflection of Consciousness आगता having attained स्वप्ने in dream वासनाः ideas कल्पयेत् imagines बोधे in the waking state अक्षैः with respect to the sense-organs बहिः external विषयान् objects कल्पयेत् imagines.

11. The inner[1] organ (mind) which is itself but a modification (वृत्तिः) identifying[2] itself with the reflection of Consciousness imagines (various) ideas[3] in the dream. And the same inner organ (identifying itself with the body) imagines[4] objects external to itself in the waking state with respect to the sense-organs.

[1] *Inner organ*—This comprises mind (मनस्), mind-stuff (चित्तः), intellect (बुद्धिः) and egoism (अहंकारः).

[2] *Identify*—It is like the identification of the heat (fire) with the iron ball.

[3] *Ideas*—The ideas of the ego and the non-ego as well as their mutual relationship.

[4] *Imagines*—We remember our dream experiences in the waking state. The dream experiences which have the same nature as the waking ones are known to be internal only in the waking state. The waking experiences are also mere ideas or thoughts of the perceiving mind.

XII

The real nature of the inner organ (अन्तःकरण) is thus described:—

मनोऽहंकृत्युपादानं लिंगमेकं जडात्मकं ।
अवस्थात्रयमन्वेति जायते म्रियते तथा ॥ १२ ॥

मनोऽहंकृत्युपादानं the material cause of mind and egoism एकं one जडात्मकं of the nature of insentiency लिंगं subtle अवस्थात्रयं the three states अन्वेति attains तथा similarly जायते is born म्रियते dies.

12. The subtle[1] body which is the material cause of the mind and egoism is one[2] and of the nature[3] of insentiency. It moves[4] in the three states and is born and it dies.

[1] *Subtle body*—This is the same as the Antahkarana and is called *lingam*, because it enables the Jīva or the embodied being to *realise* Brahman. This subtle body has been described in other Vedāntic texts as composed of seventeen parts, *viz.*, five organs of perception, five organs of knowledge, five modifications of prāna, mind (मनस्) and intellect (बुद्धिः).

[2] *One*—The subtle body (लिंगं) and the *Antahkarana* are really one and identical, though from the empirical standpoint they appear as different. Like the water and the wave the *Antahkarana* (वृत्तिमान्) and the ideas which manifest themselves as powers of knowledge and activity (ज्ञानशक्ति and क्रियाशक्ति which are only वृत्ति or the modifications of the mind) are identical.

[3] *Nature etc.*—It is because the *Antahkarana* is the modification of the Avidyā which is of the nature of insentiency. It appears as sentient on account of its identification with the reflection of Consciousness (चिदाभासः).

[4] *Moves etc.*—The identification with the three states as well as birth, death etc. can be predicated of the ego only and not of Ātman or Self who is unassociated with these conditions.

XIII

The existence of the material world is a matter of indubitable experience. The question arises, what is its cause? Brahman, which is beyond all causal relations, cannot create it. Therefore the scriptures postulate Māyā as the cause of the appearance of the universe. This Māyā is extremely illusive. It cannot be described either as real or unreal.

The best way to describe Māyā is to explain its two aspects, which is done in the following sloka:—

शक्तिद्वयं हि मायाया विक्षेपावृतिरूपकं ।
विक्षेपशक्तिर्लिंगादि ब्रह्माण्डांतं जगत्सृजेत् ॥ १३ ॥

3

मायायाः of Māyā विक्षेपावृतिरूपकं of the nature of projecting (creating) and veiling शक्तिद्वयं two powers हि without doubt (अस्ति exists) विक्षेपशक्तिः projecting power लिङ्गादि ब्रह्माण्डान्तं from the subtle body to the (gross) universe जगत् world सृजेत् creates.

13. Two powers, undoubtedly, are predicated of Māyā, *viz.*, those of projecting[1] and veiling. The projecting power creates everything from the subtle[2] body to the gross universe.

[1] *Projecting*—This leads one to think of the pure and attributeless Ātman to be Viswa, Taijasa and Prājna, associated with the experiences of waking, dream and deep sleep. It is, again, under the influence of this aspect of Māyā that the non-dual Brahman appears as the manifested manifold.

[2] *Subtle body*—This body consists of seventeen parts. See *ante*, sloka 12.

XIV

From the relative standpoint, Brahman is pointed out as the cause of the universe because the mind seeks a cause. That Brahman is, really speaking, not the cause, can be seen from the following sloka which describes the true nature of creation :—

सृष्टिर्नाम ब्रह्मरूपे सच्चिदानंदवस्तुनि ।
अब्धौ फेनादिवत्सर्वनामरूपप्रसारणा ॥ १४ ॥

ब्रह्मरूपे of the nature of Brahman सच्चिदानन्द-वस्तुनि in the entity which is Existence-Consciousness-Bliss अब्धौ in the ocean फेनादिवत् like foams etc. सर्वनामरूपप्रसारणा the manifesting of all names and forms सृष्टिः creation नाम is called.

14. The manifesting[1] of all names[2] and forms[3] in the entity[4] which is Existence-[5]Consciousness-Bliss and which is the same as Brahman, like[6] the foams etc. in the ocean, is known as creation.[7]

[1] *Manifesting*—This manifestation is due to the projecting power of Māyā which is potential in Brahman from the causal standpoint.

[2] *Names*—By which things are designated.

[3] *Forms*—That which is expressed by a name. Both names and forms are mere forms of thought as can be understood by the analysis of names and forms experienced in dream, which are nothing but the modifications of the mind.

[4] *Entity*—Reality is not a void or negation as the Buddhists contend. The appearance of the manifold cannot be based on an Absolute negation. In empirical experience, every appearance has a positive substratum. The illusion of names and forms appears from, and disappears in, Brahman.

[5] *Existence etc.*—These are not positive attributes of Brahman, which cannot be described by word or thought. Words etc. can describe only what is perceived in the perceptual world.

[6] *Like etc.*—This illustration is for the purpose of showing the indescribable nature of creation. Foams, waves, bubbles etc. are not separate from the ocean, because all these are made of the same stuff

as water. Again, they are not identical with the ocean, because we do make a distinction between the ocean and the waves, etc. Similarly the manifested manifold is not separate from Brahman, as the Sruti says, because no separate universe can be conceived of, which, according to the Sruti, is not of the nature of Existence-Consciousness-Bliss. Again, from the Sruti we know Brahman as separate from the world, which we perceive to be gross, solid, extended in time and space, etc. This appearance of the universe as separate from Brahman is due to Māyā.

[7] *Creation*—Vedānta explains the origin of the universe by saying that it is the unfolding of Brahman through Its inscrutable power, called Māyā. As the rope appears in the form of the snake, or as the ocean appears in the form of foams, waves etc. or as the sleeping man appears to be living in a dream world, so also Brahman appears in the form of the world. From the causal standpoint, Brahman is both the material and efficient cause of the world.

XV

Now is described the veiling power of Māyā:—

अंतर्दृग्दृश्ययोर्भेदं बहिश्च ब्रह्मसर्गयोः ।
आवृणोत्यपरा शक्तिस्सा संसारस्य कारणम् ॥ १५ ॥

अपरा शक्तिः the other power (of Māyā) अन्तः within दृक् दृश्ययोः (भेदं) (the distinction) between the seer and the seen (objects) बहिः outside च also ब्रह्मसर्गयोः (भेदं) (the distinction) between Brahman and the created universe आवृणोति conceals सा this power संसारस्य of the phenomenal universe कारणं cause (भवति is).

15. The other[1] power (of Māyā) conceals the distinction between the perceiver[2] and the perceived objects[3] which are cognized within the body as well as the distinction between Brahman[4] and the phenomenal[5] universe which is perceived outside (one's own body). This[6] *power* (शक्ति) is the cause of the phenomenal universe.

[1] *Other power*—It is known as the Āvarana Śakti (the veiling power) of Māyā.

[2] *Perceiver*—The. Witness (साक्षी) which is the cause of the immediate perception of "I" (see *ante*, sloka 1). It considers itself as the enjoyer etc. by identifying itself with the gross and the subtle body. Really speaking, it is the relationless Ātman.

[3] *Objects*—It includes everything from the empirical ego to the gross body. The Sākshin is distinct from the perceived objects. But the veiling power of Māyā does not enable us to see the distinction and therefore the Sākshin appears to have identified itself with the empirical ego, mind, sense-organs etc.

[4] *Brahman*—Brahman is said to be of the nature of Existence-Consciousness-Bliss. But through the veiling power of Māyā It seems to have identified Itself with names and forms and thus appears as objects of enjoyment.

[5] *Phenomenal*—This is a mere appearance like that of silver in the mother-o'-pearl.

[6] *This etc.*—From the highest standpoint there is neither creation nor dissolution. Non-dual Brahman alone is and always exists. The appearance of the manifold is due to the veiling power of Māyā which conceals the real non-dual nature of Brahman and

presents the appearance of the variegated universe. It is just like perceiving dream objects with which the sleeper at that time is in no way connected. From the subjective standpoint a man becomes a world-bound creature on account of the identification of the seer with the mind, sense-organs etc. (object). Ignorance of the distinction between the subject and the object is the cause of one's sufferings in the world.

Though it is a custom with the Vedāntic writers to describe the veiling power (Āvarana Śakti) as prior to the projecting power (Vikshēpa Śakti), the author of this treatise makes here a departure. Strictly speaking, the Āvarana Śakti cannot be said to precede the Vikshēpa Śakti or *vice versa*. For, the effects of both are seen simultaneously. One cannot be conceived of without the other.

XVI

That Māyā is the cause of the appearance of the universe has already been stated. The question now arises: what is the nature of Jiva who suffers by the law of transmigration? It is the illusory characteristic of the universe that is described below with a view to discuss later on the real nature of Jiva:—

साक्षिणः पुरतो भाति लिंगं देहेन संयुतम् ।
चितिच्छाया समावेशाज्जीवस्स्याद्व्यावहारिकः ॥ १६ ॥

साक्षिणः of the Witness, पुरतः in immediate proximity लिङ्गं the subtle body देहेन with the (physical) body संयुतं related भाति shines. (That subtle body) चितिच्छायासमावेशात् on account of its being affected by the reflection of Consciousness व्यावहारिकः empirical जीवः embodied self स्यात् becomes.

16. The subtle body (Lingam) which exists in close proximity to the Witness(Sākshin) identifying itself with the gross body becomes the embodied empirical[1] self, on account of its being affected by the reflection of Consciousness.

[1] *Empirical self*—It is that which thinks itself as the agent, enjoyer etc. It is this Jiva that appears to die and be re born etc. But the Sākshin or Ātman is birthless, deathless, immutable and without attributes.

XVII

A doubt arises here. The embodied self is unreal and hence liberation is not possible for it. Again the Sākshin is ever free; therefore no liberation is necessary for it. There is no third entity for whom the scriptures, pointing to liberation, can be prescribed. Therefore scriptures become futile. The following stanza removes this doubt by showing that the idea of the embodied self is falsely superimposed upon the Sākshin or the Witness.

अस्य जीवत्वमारोपात्साक्षिण्यप्यवभासते ।
आवृतौ तु विनष्टायां भेदे भातेऽपयाति तत् ॥ १७ ॥

अस्य of this (the empirical self) जीवत्वं the nature of being a Jiva आरोपात् through superimposition साक्षिणि in the Sākshin अपि also अवभासते

appears आवृतौ of the veiling power तु but विनष्टायां by the annihilation, भेदे the difference भाते having become clear तत् that (the idea of being Jiva), अपयाति disappears.

17. The character of an embodied self appears through false[1] superimposition in the Sākshin[2] also[3]. With the disappearance of the veiling power, the distinction[4] (between the seer and the object) becomes clear and with it the Jiva character of the Sākshin (Witness) disappears.[5]

[1] *False superimposition*—This is due to the projecting powers of Māyā.

[2] *Sākshin*— Thereby the Witness appears as the world-bound Jiva.

[3] *Also*—Though the Sākshin is ever free from all taint of worldliness.

[4] *Distinction*—Through Knowledge one realizes that the Sākshin is ever free from worldliness and is the eternal seer and all other ideas, from the empirical ego to the body, are mere objects and hence negatable.

[5] *Disappears*—This is possible only through Knowledge which one acquires from the study and the understanding of the scriptures. Hence scriptures are not futile.

XVIII

As in the case of the subject itself the Sākshin, through false identification, appears to have become the Jiva, so also Brahman appears to be identified with the objective universe.

तथा सर्गब्रह्मणोश्च भेदमावृत्य तिष्ठति ।
या शक्तिस्तद्वशाद्ब्रह्म विकृतत्वेन भासते ॥ १८ ॥

तथा similarly या which शक्तिः power सर्गब्रह्मणोः of Brahman and phenomenal universe भेदं distinction आवृत्य concealing तिष्ठति exists तद्वशात् through its influence ब्रह्म Brahman विकृतत्वेन as being of the nature of modification भासते appears.

18. Similarly,[1] Brahman, through the influence of the power[2] that conceals the distinction between It[3] and the phenomenal universe, appears as endowed with the attributes[4] of change.

[1] *Similarly*—As in the case of the Witness and the object, with reference to the individual self.

[2] *Power*—The concealing power of Māyā (आवरणशक्ति).

[3] *It*—The real nature of Brahman is that It is without attributes.

[4] *Attributes*—The six attributes of the manifested manifold, *viz.*, birth, existence, growth, change, decay and annihilation. Under the influence of Māyā, Brahman appears to possess these attributes and to be identified with the world.

XIX

When that veiling power is destroyed, the distinction between Brahman and the phenomenal universe becomes clear and then the changes etc. attributed to Brahman disappear.

अत्राप्यावृतिनाशेन विभाति ब्रह्मसर्गयोः ।
भेदस्तयोर्विकारस्स्यात्सर्गे न ब्रह्मणि कचित् ॥ १९. ॥

अत्र अपि in this case also आवृतिनाशेन with the destruction of the veiling power ब्रह्मसर्गयोः of Brahman and the phenomenal universe भेदः distinction विभाति becomes clear ततः therefore सर्गे in the phenomenal universe विकारः change स्यात् exists न not ब्रह्मणि in Brahman कचित् ever (विकारः स्यात् change exists).

19. In[1] this case also, the distinction between Brahman and the phenomenal universe becomes clear with[2] the disappearance of the veiling power. Therefore change[3] is perceived in the phenomenal universe, but never in Brahman.

[1] *In etc.*—As in the case of the individual self.

[2] *With etc.*—As the result of the knowledge of the non-dual Brahman.

[3] *Change etc.*—Whose essential characteristics are birth, growth, decay etc.

In the foregoing stanzas we have seen, following the methods of agreement and difference, that the word "त्वं" ("Thou" in the Vedic statement, "That Thou Art") indicates the Witness (Sākshin) which is immutable and changeless and that the word "तत्" indicates Brahman which is unrelated to the phenomena. The attributes generally associated with "Thou" and "That" are mere appearances and hence unreal.

XX

Now is shown the identity of "Thou" and "That":—

अस्ति भाति प्रियं रूपं नामचेत्यंशपञ्चकम् ।

आद्यत्रयं ब्रह्मरूपं जगद्रूपं ततो द्वयम् ॥ २० ॥

अस्ति (it) exists भाति (it) shines (becomes cognizable) प्रियं (it is) dear रूपं form नाम name च इति अंशपञ्चकं all these five aspects (characterize every entity). आद्यत्रयं the first three (are) ब्रह्मरूपं characteristics of Brahman ततः the next द्वयं two जगद्रूपं characteristics of the universe.

20. Every entity has five characteristics, *viz.*, existence, cognizability,[1] attractiveness, form and name. Of these, the first three belong[2] to Brahman and the next[3] two to the world.

[1] *Cognizability*—That which makes one aware of the existence of an object.

[2] *Belong to etc.*—These three characteristics correspond to Sat, Chit, and Ānanda.

[3] *Next two*—Names and forms are the chief characteristics of Māyā.

XXI

The meaning of the preceding sloka is made clearer in the following by the methods of agreement and difference:—

खवाय्वग्निजलोर्वीषु देवतिर्यङ्नरादिषु ।

अभिन्नास्सच्चिदानंदाः भिद्येते रूपनामनी ॥ २१ ॥

खवाय्वग्निजलोर्वीषु in the Ākāsha (ether), air, fire, water and earth देवतिर्यङ्नरादिषु in gods, animals and men सच्चिदानंदाः (the attributes of) Existence, Consciousness and Bliss अभिन्नाः common features रूपनामनी forms and names भिद्यंते differ.

21. The attributes of Existence, Consciousness and Bliss are equally[1] present in the Ākāsha (ether), air, fire, water and earth as well as in gods, animals and men etc. Names and forms make[2] one differ from the other.

[1] *Equally etc.*—All objects such as a pot, a picture etc. have these common features. These are the universal characteristics.

[2] *Make etc.*—We distinguish one object from another only by their names and forms. Names and forms are characteristics of the individual and hence relative. Even after the negation of names and forms, there exists the common substratum whose nature is Existence-Consciousness-Bliss (Absolute).

XXII

Thus following the methods of agreement and difference, we get the implied meaning of "तत्" ("That") and "त्वं" ("Thou") which points to the Satchidānanda Brahman. Therefore Brahman is identical with the Jiva. But one should practise concentration (Samādhi) in order to strengthen this conviction. The methods of Samādhi are described below :—

उपेक्ष्य नामरूपे द्वे सच्चिदानंदतत्परः ।
समाधिं सर्वदा कुर्याद्धृदये वाऽथवा बहिः ॥ २२ ॥

नामरूपे (to) name and form द्वे two उपेक्ष्य being indifferent सच्चिदानंदतत्परः (सन्) being devoted to Satchidānanda हृदये वा either in the heart, अथवा or बहिः outside सर्वदा always समाधिं concentration कुर्यात् should practise.

22. Having[1] become indifferent to name and form and being devoted to Satchidānanda[2], one should always practise concentration[3] either within the heart[4] or outside.[5]

[1] *Having etc.*—Names and forms are impermannte, because they appear and disappear. Though names and forms give the direct meaning (वाच्यार्थ) of "That" (तत्) and "Thou" (त्वं), yet they are negatable as found in deep sleep.

[2] *Satchidānanda*—This is the implied meaning (लक्ष्यार्थ) of all objects. The characteristics of Existence, Consciousness and Bliss are universal and therefore they form the common features of the substratum of all objects comprehended by "That" and "Thou". Therefore these aspects alone, being permanent, as distinguished from names and forms, are worthy of concentration.

[3] *Concentration*—Concentration or Samādhi means the one-pointedness of the mind by which the student feels his steady identity with Brahman.

[4] *Heart*—Heart is pointed out, for the facility of concentration, as the seat of Paramātman.

[5] *Outside*—That is, concentration can be practised through the help of any external object, such as a

word, sound, image or any other symbol. These two modes of concentration are meant for different temperaments.

XXIII

Samādhi with its twofold division is described in the following seven stanzas. Concentration *within* the heart is described in the three following :—

सविकल्पो निर्विकल्पः समाधिर्द्विविधो हृदि ।
दृश्यशब्दानुवेधेन सविकल्पः पुनर्द्विधा ॥ २३ ॥

सविकल्पः in which the ideas are present, निर्विकल्पः in which ideas do not exist हृदि (to be practised) within the heart समाधिः concentration (इति) द्विविधः of two kinds सविकल्पः समाधिः concentration in which ideas are present दृश्यशब्दानुवेधेन according to its association with a cognizable object or with a sound (as an object) पुनः again द्विधा (are) of two kinds.

23. Two kinds of Samādhi to be practised in the heart (within one's self) are known as Savikalpa[1] and Nirvikalpa.[2] Savikalpa Samādhi is again divided into two classes, according to its association with a cognizable object or a sound (as an object).

[1] *Savikalpa*—In this Samādhi, the practitioner concentrates his mind on Brahman without completely losing such distinctions as the knower, knowledge and the known. This is the initial step in the practice of concentration.

[2] *Nirvikalpa*—In this Samādhi the practitioner makes himself free from all thought of distinctions, as the knower, knowledge and the known.

XXIV

Now is described the Samādhi (Savikalpa) in which concentration is associated with an object.

कामाद्याश्चित्तगा दृश्यास्तत्साक्षित्वेन चेतनम् ।
ध्यायेद्दृश्यानुविद्धोऽयं समाधिस्सविकल्पकः ॥ २४ ॥

चित्तगाः centred in the mind कामाद्याः desire etc. दृश्याः (cognizable) objects चेतनं Consciousness तत्साक्षित्वेन as their Witness ध्यायेत् should meditate अयं this दृश्यानुविद्धः (is) combined with cognizable objects सविकल्पकः in which ideas are present समाधिः concentration.

24. Desire[1] etc. centred[2] in the mind are to be treated as (cognizable) objects. Meditate on Consciousness[3] as their Witness.[4] This is what is called Savikalpa Samādhi associated with (cognizable) objects.

[1] *Desire*—See *ante*, 4.

[2] *Centred etc.*—Because they are the modifications of the mind. They disappear with the disappearance of the mind as in deep sleep. Therefore, they have got nothing to do with Ātman.

[3] *Consciousness*—It means Ātman, that is, the Witness of all these mental modifications.

[4] *Witness*—Because of the presence of Ātman, the mind and its modifications are seen to be active.

Then the process of the meditation is this:—Whenever any thought appears in the mind, take it to be an object and be indifferent to it. But think of the Ātman as your real nature, eternal and permanent. The object which is an idea appears and disappears. This sort of concentration is always associated with an object of thought.

XXV

Now is described a higher kind of Savikalpa Samādhi, with which some sound (object) is associated:—

असंगस्सच्चिदानंदस्स्वप्रभो द्वैतवर्जितः ।
अस्मीति शब्दविद्धोऽयं समाधिस्सविकल्पकः ॥ २५ ॥

(अहं I) असंगः unattached सच्चिदानन्दः Existence-Consciousness-Bliss स्वप्रभः self-luminous द्वैतवर्जितः free from duality अस्मि am इति अयं this शब्दविद्धः (is) associated with words सविकल्पकः समाधिः Savikalpaka Samādhi.

25. I am Existence[1]–Consciousness–Bliss, unattached,[2] self-luminous[3] and free[4] from duality. This is known as the (other kind of) Savikalpa Samādhi associated with sound (object).

[1] *Existence etc.*—Sat, Chit and Ānanda are the natural characteristics of Ātman.

[2] *Unattached*—Unrelated to Chitta or mind whose functions are seen as desire, volition etc. Ātman is also unattached to virtue and vice, weal and woe, (relative) knowledge and ignorance etc. Comp. "असंगोऽयं पुरुषः" "This Purusha is unattached."

[3] *Self-luminous*—The existence of Ātman can never be doubted even when the relative objects are absent as in deep sleep. Compare "अदृष्टं द्रष्टृ श्रुतं श्रोतृ" (बृ. उ. ३-८-११) "न दृष्टे र्द्रष्टारं पश्येः" (बृ. उ. ३-४-७). "(That Brahman) is unseen but seeing, unheard but hearing." "Thou couldst not see the Seer of sight."

[4] *Free from etc.*—Nothing else exists besides the Ātman, because Ātman is one and without a second and it has no parts and it is not of the nature of insentiency. Comp. "एकमेवाद्वितीयं" (छां. उ. ६-७-१). "He is, verily, one without a second."

While practising this concentration the practitioner thinks, "I am the Witness, the innermost Self". The object of his meditation is the non-dual Self free from the ideas of desire etc. which are foreign to Ātman. There is only a current of self-consciousness. This sort of concentration is called Savikalpaka as it is not free from ideas altogether. Such ideas as, "I am unattached," etc. are present in this Samādhi.

XXVI

Now is described the higher concentration free from all ideas whatsoever :—

स्वानुभूतिरसावेशाद् दृश्यशब्दावुपेक्ष्यतु ।
निर्विकल्पस्समाधिस्स्यान्निवातास्थितदीपवत् ॥ २६ ॥

तु but स्वानुभूतिरसावेशात् on account of complete absorption in the bliss of realization of the Self दृश्यशब्दौ both the perceived objects and sounds उपेक्ष्य being indifferent to निवातस्थितदीपवत् like a flame in a place free from wind, निर्विकल्पः समाधिः absorption free from (subject-object) ideas स्यात् is.

26. But[1] the Nirvikalpa Samādhi is that in which the mind[2] becomes steady like the (unflickering flame of a) light kept in a place free from wind and in which the student becomes indifferent to both[3] objects and sounds on account[4] of his complete absorption in the bliss of the realization of the Self.

[1] *But*—The Nirvikalpa Samādhi is here distinguished from the Savikalpa Samādhi as described in the foregoing slokas.

[2] *Mind etc.*—Through the constant practice of the Savikalpa Samādhi, mind becomes free from all distractions which is the result of attachment to sense-objects. Therefore he, then, becomes competent to practise Nirvikalpa Samādhi in which the mind becomes steady like the unflickering flame of a candle kept in a windless place. Compare—

"यथा दीपो निवातस्थो नेङ्गते सोपमा स्मृता ।

योगिनो यतचित्तस्य युञ्जतो योगमात्मनः ॥ (गीता ६. १९)

"As a lamp in a spot unsheltered from the wind, does not flicker,—even such has been the simile used for a Yogi of subdued mind, practising concentration in the Self."

[3] *Both etc.*—These are associated with concentration in the Savikalpa Samādhi. Desires etc. are the cognizable objects and "I am unattached" etc. are sound (objects) or ideas.

[4] *On account etc.*—The word *Anubhūti*, in the text, means "Highest Consciousness" or "Self". Comp.

"यानुभूतिरजामेया स्वनंतानंदविग्रहा ।

महदादिजगन्माया चित्रभित्तिर्नमामि ताम् ॥" (इष्टसिद्धि, ७८)

"I bow to that innermost (Subjective) Self, birthless, incomprehensible, infinite, the embodiment of Bliss and the background of the World, created by Mahat etc. and painted by ignorance (Māyā)."

The word 'Rasa' means the Supreme Self or the nature of the Highest Bliss. Comp. "रसो वै सः। रसꣳ ह्येवायं लब्ध्वानन्दी भवति" (तै. उ. २.७-१). "He is the Rasa, flavour, for only after perceiving a flavour can any one become blessed."

The word *Āvesa* means complete absorption. Or it may mean the 'manifestation' of the Supreme Bliss in the heart as the index of success in the Savikalpa Samādhi. Another meaning of the word is 'coming' (प्रवेश) from all directions (आ) of bliss. Still another meaning is the 'possession' *i.e.* the practitioner becomes possessed, as it were, by the bliss of self-realization and can no longer control himself.

The Nirvikalpa Samādhi is the highest kind of concentration in which the practitioner realises his real Self. In this Samādhi the functions of the mind are stopped and the practitioner experiences the Highest Bliss. Compare—

"प्रशांतवृत्तिकं चित्तं परमानंददीपकम् ।
असंप्रज्ञातनामायं समाधिर्योगिनां प्रियः" ॥

(मुक्तिकोपनिषत्, ७-५४)

"The mind, with the utter quiescence of modifications conferring upon one Supreme Bliss, is said to be Asamprajñāta Samādhi that is dear unto the Yogīs."

This Samādhi is characterized by the absence of the knowledge of the subject-object relationship. Apparently it is like that state of calmness and tranquillity which pervades a stone, because in the

Nirvikalpa Samādhi the mind stops its functioning. But it should not be mistaken for stupor or deep sleep in which state alone one experiences absence of duality. The difference between deep sleep and Nirvikalpa Samādhi is that in the former state there is no knowledge of Self, but in the latter there exists no feeling of not knowing the Self, because in the Nirvikalpa Samādhi one becomes identified with the ever-Conscious Ātman. Compare—

"संशांतसर्वसंकल्पा या शिलांतरिव स्थितिः ।
जाड्यनिद्राविनिर्मुक्ता सा स्वरूपास्थितिः स्मृता ॥"

(वासिष्ठरामायण, उत्पत्तिप्रकरण, ११७–९)

"The state in which all desires completely disappear which is (quiescent) like the interior of a stone, but which is not characterized by swoon or deep sleep is admitted as the real nature of Ātman."

Nirvikalpa Samādhi which is identical with the Highest Knowledge can be attained only as a result of discrimination between the real and the unreal. After this discrimination, the student becomes indifferent to everything of the relative world. Comp. तत्परं पुरुषख्यातेर्गुणवैतृष्ण्यम् (*Pātanjali Sutra*, Samādhi Pāda, 16). "That is extreme non-attachment, which gives up even the qualities and comes from the Knowledge of (the real nature of) the Purusha."

This Samādhi is possible only for him who has become established in complete renunciation. Comp. "तीव्रसंवेगानामासन्नः" (समाधिलाभः) (पा. सू., समाधिपाद, ७१). "Success is speedy for the extremely energetic."

In this Samādhi one becomes free from all thoughts or ideas but infilled with Supreme Bliss. Compare—

"अन्तश्शून्यो बहिश्शून्यश्शून्यकुंभ इवांबरे ।
अन्तःपूर्णो बहिःपूर्णः पूर्णकुंभ इवार्णवे ॥

(वासिष्ठरामायण, निर्वाणपूर्वप्रकरण, १२६-६८)

" It is just like an empty pitcher placed in the sky, having nothing inside and outside; and again, it is just like a full pitcher placed in the sea, full (of water) both inside and outside.

XXVII

By the practice of Samādhi described above the practitioner realises his own Self which is of the nature of Existence-Consciousness-Bliss. But this concentration can also be practised with the help of any object in the external world. By such concentration one can realise the nature of Brahman and creation. Brahman and Self are identical :—

हृदीव बाह्यदेशेऽपि यस्मिन्कस्मिंश्च वस्तुनि ।
समाधिराद्यस्सन्मात्रान्नामरूपपृथक्कृतिः ॥ २७ ॥

हृदीव as in the heart बाह्यदेशेऽपि in the external region as well यस्मिन् कस्मिन्श्च वस्तुनि in any object whatsoever आद्य of the first kind समाधिस्स्यात् concentration is possible सः that (Samādhi) सन्मात्रात् from the Pure Existence (which is Brahman) नामरूपपृथक्कृतिः the separation of names and forms.

27. The first[1] kind of Samādhi is possible with the help of any external[2] object as it is with the help of an internal[3] object. In that Samādhi the name and form are separated[4] from what is Pure Existence[5] (Brahman).

[1] *First kind etc.—i.e.* the Savikalpa Samādhi with the help of an object (दृश्यानुविद्धः).

[2] *External*—By concentration on such external objects, as the sun etc.

[3] *Internal etc.*—Such as desire etc.

[4] *Separated*—Names and forms on account of their appearance and disappearance are negatable. This is done by concentration on the Satchidānanda factor of an entity.

[5] *Pure Existence*—The Existence aspect of an object can never be negated.

We have seen in the 24th stanza that concentration can be practised with the help of an object perceived internally. Similar concentration can be practised with the help of an external object also. Every object, as we have seen, has three unchangeable aspects, namely, Existence, Visibility, and Attractiveness. The two other changing aspects are names and forms. The practitioner should concentrate his mind on Pure Existence which is the same as Brahman and dissociate himself from the changing aspects of name and form.

XXVIII

Now is described the other kind of Savikalpaka Samādhi (शब्दानुविद्ध) associated with sound (object) to be practised with the help of an external object:—

अखंडैकरसं वस्तु साच्चिदानन्दलक्षणम् ।

इत्यविच्छिन्नचिंतेयं समाधिर्मध्यमो भवेत् ॥ २८ ॥

अखंडैकरसं of the same nature (always) and unlimited (by time, space etc.) सच्चिदानन्दलक्षणं characterised by Existence-Consciousness-Bliss (यत्) वस्तु entity (तदेव ब्रह्म that is Brahman) इति

इयं अविच्छिन्नाचिन्ता such uninterrupted reflection मध्यमः middle, समाधिः concentration भवेत् is.

28. The entity which[1] is (always) of the same nature and unlimited (by time, space etc.) and which is characterised by Existence-Consciousness-Bliss, is verily Brahman. Such uninterrupted reflection is called the intermediate[2] absorption, that is, the Savikalpaka Samādhi associated with sound (object).

[1] *Which is etc.*—Which remains the same, that is, immutable in the past, present and future and which is not limited by time, space etc.

[2] *Intermediate*—Because it is superior to the Samādhi described in the foregoing Sloka and inferior to the Nirvikalpa Samādhi.

This Samādhi is similar to the one described in Sloka 25. The only difference is that it is associated with an external (objective) idea whereas the other one is associated with an internal (subjective) idea.

XXIX

Now is described the Nirvikalpaka Samādhi which can be practised by following the objective method :—

स्तब्धीभावो रसास्वादात्तृतीयः पूर्ववन्मतः ।
एतैस्समाधिभिष्षड्भिर्नयेत्कालं निरंतरम् ॥ २९ ॥

रसास्वादात् from the experience of Bliss स्तब्धीभावः insensibility (to external objects) पूर्ववत् as in the previous instance तृतीयः (समाधिः)

the third kind of Samādhi मतः described (पंडितानां by the teachers) एतैः षड्भिः समाधिभिः by the help of these six kinds of Samādhi निरन्तरं always कालं time नयेत् should spend.

29. The insensibility[1] of the mind (to external objects) as[2] before, on account of the experience[3] of Bliss, is designated as the third kind of Samādhi (Nirvikalpaka). The practitioner should uninterruptedly[4] spend his time in these six[5] kinds of Samādhi.

[1] *Insensibility*—This shows that the mind is completely absorbed in the contemplation of Brahman.

[2] *As before*—As in the case of Samādhi described in the twenty-sixth Sloka ; here also the practitioner attains the Nirvikalpaka Samādhi by merging the entire illusory phenomena in Brahman and by being indifferent to the manifested manifold (दृश्य) and such ideas as "indivisible" (अखंडः), of the same nature (एकरसः) etc. Concentration becomes steady like the unflickering flame of a candle in a place free from wind.

[3] *Experience etc.*—This bliss is due to the knowledge of Brahman whom the scriptures describe as an entity of Bliss. The Self (subject) is identical with Brahman. In the subjective concentration, the Self which is the Witness of all mental modifications is identical with Brahman. Otherwise such concentration, without a substratum, becomes a mere mental abstraction and ends in nihilism. Again, in objective concentration, Brahman, the unchanging entity in all perceived objects, because of its all-pervasive nature, is identical with the Self (subject). As the knowledge of Brahman is associated with bliss so also the knowledge of Self is accompanied by Bliss Eternal.

[4] *Uninterruptedly*—This Samādhi should be practised uninterruptedly for a long time. Then only can the practitioner be firmly established in supreme knowledge. *Cf.* (सतु) "दीर्घकालनैरंतर्यसत्कारसेवितोदृढभूमिः" (पा. सू., समाधिपाद, ७४). "It becomes firmly grounded by long, constant efforts with great love (for the end to be attained)."

[5] *Six*—That is, three subjective and three objective.

XXX

As a result of the constant practice of Samādhi, described above, it becomes subsequently quite natural and spontaneous. Then the student realises Brahman everywhere.

देहाभिमाने गळिते विज्ञाते परमात्मनि ।

यत्र यत्र मनो याति तत्र तत्र समाधयः ॥ ३० ॥

देहाभिमाने the attachment to the body गळिते with the disappearance of परमात्मनि the Supreme Self विज्ञाते (सति) with the realization of यत्रयत्र to whatever objects मनः mind याति goes तत्रतत्र there समाधयः absorptions (भवन्ति are).

30. With the disappearance of the attachment[1] to the body and with the realization of the Supreme Self, to whatever object[2] the mind is directed one experiences Samādhi.[3]

[1] *Attachment etc.*—On account of such attachment to body, a being feels that he is a man, a Brahmin, a so and so, etc. Following the process of enquiry laid down in Vedānta, the student realises that all

internal entities from the empirical ego to the body are only objects and the subject (Self) is the Witness. Therefore, he ceases to identify himself as attached to the objects, knowing that appearance and disappearance are their inevitable nature. Similarly, by an analysis of the external world he realises that Brahman is the only permanent entity in the universe, while names and forms are changing phenomena. Therefore the practitioner becomes indifferent to the internal and external objects and fixes his mind on Brahman which is identical with the Self.

[2] *Objects*—As perceived by the senses.

[3] *Samādhi*—That is, as a result of constant practice of Yogic Samādhi, as described above, for a long time and with the help of the knowledge of Truth, the practitioner realises all objects, internal and external, as Brahman. Even the names and forms which appear to the ignorant as devoid of reality are looked upon by the Jnāni as ever existent Brahman. He sees everywhere Brahman only. The knowledge of Brahman which is at first attainable by effort becomes, later on, quite spontaneous and natural.

XXXI

Now is described the result of this supreme realization in the language of the *Mundaka Upanishad* (2-8) :—

भिद्यते हृदयग्रंथिः छिद्यंते सर्वसंशयाः ।
क्षीयंते चास्यकर्माणि तस्मिन्दृष्टे परावरे ॥ ३१ ॥

तस्मिन् परावरे Him who is high and low दृष्टे by beholding हृदयग्रन्थिः fetters of the heart भिद्यते is broken सर्वसंशयाः all doubts छिद्यन्ते are solved

अस्य His कर्माणि च all works (and their effects) क्षीयन्ते wear away.

31. By[1] beholding Him who[2] is high and low, the fetters[3] of the heart are broken, all[4] doubts are solved and all[5] his Karmas (activities and their effects) wear away.

[1] *By beholding Him*—That is, by realising Brahman throughout the manifested manifold.

[2] *Who is high and low*—The word high (पर) signifies Brahmā, what is known as cause of the universe. The word low (अपर) signifies the universe etc. which are the effects. It is the non-dual Turīya Brahman alone that exists everywhere, both in the cause and in the effect.

[3] *Fetters etc.*—This denotes ideas of agency etc. which are falsely superimposed on the Self. This is due to ignorance.

[4] *All doubts*—That is, the doubts regarding the nature of Self.

[5] *All his Karmas etc.*—For a Jnāni the accumulated works (संचितकर्म) as well as fresh works (आगामिकर्म) do not yield any result. Only the fructescent works (प्रारब्धकर्म), as a result of which a man has got his present body, continue to produce their result. This work yields its result so long as the body lasts. But this explanation is offered only from the standpoint of the ignorant who see even a Jnāni subject to disease, misery, hunger, thirst etc. But a Jnāni who has made himself quite free from the body-idea does not feel the effect of any Karma. For him all works and their effects are non-existent. Comp. "अशरीरं वावसंतं न प्रियाप्रिये स्पृशतः" (छां. उ. ८-१७-१). "(But) when he is free of the body, then neither pleasure nor pain touches him."

He who realises Brahman attains liberation (मुक्ति) which is the highest objective of life. Compare the following Sruti passages :—

"ब्रह्म वेद ब्रह्मैव भवति" (मुं. उ. ३-२-९)

"He who knows Brahman, verily, becomes Brahman."

"ब्रह्मविदाप्नोति परम्" (तै. उ. २-१-१)

"The knower of Brahman attains the Highest."

"तरति शोकमात्मवित्" (छां. उ. ७-१-३)

"The knower of Self goes beyond grief."

"अभयं वै जनक प्राप्तोऽसि" (बृ. उ. ४-१-४)

"Oh ! Janaka ! You have attained fearlessness."

"एतावदरे खल्वमृतत्वमिति" (बृ. उ. ४-५-१५)

"Oh, (Maitreyi), thus far goes immortality."

"तमेव विदित्वा अतिमृत्युमेति" (श्वे. उ. ३-८, ६-१५)

"Knowing it (Self) one goes beyond death."

"यत्रत्वाऽस्य सर्वमात्मैवाऽभूत्" (बृ. उ. २-४-१३)

"When the Self only is all this."

XXXII

We have seen the method prescribed in this treatise for the realization of the Highest Truth. By following this method the student understands the real significance of "That" and "Thou" and ultimately realises that identity. All these have been described in their proper places. The various helps for the attainment of such knowledge have been dealt with as well as the result of the knowledge of identity. The treatise may be said to be completed here. But a doubt may still arise in the mind of the student. What is the nature of Jiva? If the Witness (Sākshin) is really Brahman, then He cannot be Jiva. And if He is Jiva, then He cannot be Brahman. In any case, the teaching is of no use. Therefore, it is necessary to explain to the student the real nature of Jiva.

The student will be told in the following slokas that the Jiva in reality is Sākshin and identical with Brahman. The Sākshin considers itself to be Jiva owing to his identification with the Upādhis:—

अवच्छिन्नश्चिदाभासस्तृतीयः स्वप्नकल्पितः ।
विज्ञेयस्त्रिविधोजीवस्तत्राद्यः पारमार्थिकः ॥ ३२ ॥

अवच्छिन्नः limited चिदाभासः unreal presentation of Consciousness तृतीयः स्वप्नकल्पितः the third is as imagined in dream इति त्रिविधः these three kinds जीवः embodied being विज्ञेयः should be known तत्र among them आद्यः the first one पारमार्थिकः (is) the real nature (of Jiva).

32. There are three conceptions of Jiva (Consciousness), namely, as that *limited* (by) prāna etc., as that *presented* (in the mind) and the third one Consciousness as *imagined* in dream (to have assumed the forms of man etc.)

According to the first theory, Sākshin (the Seer) appears to be subject to various Upādhis (limitations) of Prāna, sense-organ, mind etc. and thus regards himself as Jiva. It is like the infinite space (Ākāsha) portions of which appear to be limited by pots etc. According to the second theory, the Consciousness (Sākshin) appears to be fallaciously presented in the mind and this presentation is known as Jiva. It is like the reflection of the sun in water. The reflection always partakes of the qualities of the medium in which it is reflected as the reflection of the sun is seen to be moving etc. with the movement of the water. Similarly, the presentation of Consciousness in the mind partakes of the qualities of the mind, such as agency, desire, volition etc. According to a third theory, the nature of Jiva is the same as the nature of various beings one sees in dream. In dream, on account of the absence of the knowledge of reality, one thinks of himself as king, god, or beggar etc. Similarly, Ātman, also, through the ignorance of its real nature, thinks of itself as man, or animal etc. According to the author of this treatise, the first theory (अवच्छिन्नवादः) tells us that the real nature of Jiva is Brahman. This view is, however, not accepted by all schools of Vedānta.

XXXIII

How is it possible for a limited entity (Jiva) to be identical with the Absolute Brahman? This is thus explained :—

अवच्छेदः कल्पितस्स्यादवच्छेद्यं तु वास्तवम् ।
तस्मिन्जीवत्वमारोपात् ब्रह्मत्वं तु स्वभावतः ॥ ३३ ॥

अवच्छेदः limitation कल्पितः स्यात् is imaginary (illusory) तु but अवच्छेद्यं what appears to be limited वास्तवं (is) real तस्मिन् in that (Brahman)

आरोपात् on account of superimposition जीवत्वं (स्यात्) the Jivahood appears तु but स्वभावतः naturally ब्रह्मत्वं (it is) of the nature of Brahman.

33. Limitation is illusory[1] but that which appears to be limited is real.[2] The Jivahood[3] (of the Self) is due to the superimposition of the illusory attributes. But really it[4] has the nature of Brahman.

[1] *Illusory*—The idea of limitation is illusory. What is the nature of the limitation that is superimposed upon Consciousness (Sākshin) which is without parts etc.? This limitation is said to be caused by Prāna etc. Ordinarily, limitation (अवच्छेदः) is seen to be of the following kinds:—A pillar is limited by the ground on which it stands. Or a part of it is covered (अवच्छेदः) by roof etc. This sort of limitation is not possible in Ātman because It is without parts. A frog is seen to be swallowed (अवच्छेदः) by the snake. But prāna etc. cannot act similarly with regard to Self; for, It is always complete, without parts, without activity and ever peaceful. *Cf.* "निष्कलं निष्क्रियं शांतं" (श्वे. उ. ६-१९) without parts, without actions, tranquil. "पूर्णमदः पूर्णमिदं" (शांतिपाठः) This is full and that is full. An elephant is seen to be trimmed (अवच्छेदः) by the will of its care-taker. But Prāna etc. cannot act likewise with regard to Ātman; for being themselves of insentient nature, Prāna etc. are subservient to Ātman. Compare "यः प्राणमंतरोयमयति" (बृ. उ. ३-१७-१६)—He who rules the breath within.

Hence no kind of limitation by Prāna etc. can be predicated of Ātman. Therefore the limitation which appears to be superimposed upon Ātman is illusory.

[2] *Real.*—Sākshin or Self is real, because it is the same everywhere and at all times.

[3] *Jivahood*—The appearance of Jiva is not possible without the association of upādhis. The following analogy of a scholiast is interesting. Rāhu always exists in the firmament. But it cannot be directly perceived except in association with the solar or the lunar disc. Similarly Sākshin also becomes an object of perception (Jiva) only in association with egoism, Prāna etc.

[4] *It is etc.*—The Sākshin is the same as Brahman It may be contended that if the idea of limitation (Jivatvam) and what limits it (Prāna etc.) be unreal, then Sākshin also (what appears to be limited) is unreal. But this contention is refuted thus:— Sākshin is not unreal because it is the same as Brahman. A woman wearing anklets, through illusion, considers her feet to be entwined by a snake. With the removal of the illusion, the snake idea vanishes: but her feet remain as they are. Similarly the illusion of limitation and what limits, is removed by Knowledge. But the Sākshin always exists.

XXXIV

That the theory of limitation (अवच्छेदवादः) explains in a better way the identity of Jiva and Brahman than the two other theories, is now described:—

अवच्छिन्नस्य जीवस्य पूर्णेन ब्रह्मणैकताम् ।
तत्त्वमस्यादिवाक्यानि जगुर्नेतरजीवयोः ॥ ३४ ॥

तत्त्वमस्यादि वाक्यानि such Vedic statements as "That Thou Art" etc. अवच्छिन्नस्य जीवस्य of the limited Jiva पूर्णेन ब्रह्मणा with Brahman that is without parts एकतां identity जगुः declare न not इतर जीवयोः with the two other Jivas.

34. Such Vedic statements[1] as "That Thou Art" etc. declare[2] the identity of partless[3] Brahman with the Jiva who appears as such from[4] the standpoint of the 'Theory of limitation' (अवच्छेदवादः). But it does not agree with the[5] other two views (of Jiva).

[1] *Vedic statements*—The four great Vedic statements which summarize the entire teachings of the Vedas are: (1) "That Thou Art" (तत्त्वमसि) ; (2) "I A Brahman" (अहं ब्रह्मास्मि); (3) "This Ātman is Brahman (अयं आत्मा ब्रह्म) ; (4) "(Pure) Consciousness is Brahman" (प्रज्ञानं ब्रह्म).

[2] *Declare etc.*—The method followed in arriv at su nclusion is what is known as भागत्यागलक्षण le- जहदजहद (लक्षणा or भागलक्षणा—a method in which the of tradictory ements on both sides are given up all their ide is recognized, noticing careful essence of b which is Chit or Pure Consc

[3] *Partless Brahman*—i.e., Pure Conscio

[4] *From the etc.*—That is, the Jiva as "Theory of limitation" which decla limited by the Upādhis or Avidy appears as Jiva.

[5] *The other etc.*—There ar of Jiva: one in which he ap and the other in which presentation of the Sāk tity of these Jivas, acc treatise, with Brahma mere imagination. theory of limitati

35. ... resenta- ... d in the ... and enjoys[2] ... Jiva. And all ... ents[3] and their ... ature of the objects ... gat (universe).

... uch as cultivation, trade, of the Vedas, spiritual practi- For, they have no re in this world or in heaven. ther, air, fire, water and earth.

5 —Various animate and inanimate objects.

Brahman can be demonstrated. But the two other Jivas are illusory. There cannot be any identity between an illusory appearance and a real entity.

XXXV

That the appearance of Jiva is due to the limitation (अवच्छेदः) superimposed upon Brahman is thus described :—

ब्रह्मण्यवस्थिता माया विक्षेपावृतिरूपिणी ।

आवृत्याखण्डतां तस्मिन् जगज्जीवौ प्रकल्पयेत् ॥ ३५ ॥

विक्षेपावृतिरूपिणी माया Māyā characterised by projection and concealment ब्रह्मणि in Brahman अवस्थिता rests तस्मिन् in Brahman अखण्डतां indivisible nature आवृत्य having concealed जगज्जीवौ the world and the Jiva, प्रकल्पयेत् imagines.

Māyā which has the double aspect of projection and concealment is in Brahman. ... Jiva and ... indivisible nature of Brahman ... theories, is Brahman) appear as the world ... being.

अवच्छिन्नस्य जीवस्य ... note. 13.

तत्त्वमस्यादिवाक्यानि जगुः ... for the cause of Māyā, ... are told that it (Māyā)

तत्त्वमस्यादि वाक्यानि. such ...

"That Thou Art" etc. अवच्छिन्नस्य

limited Jiva पूर्णेन ब्रह्मणा with Brahman ... the real nature of (Brahman) appears

without parts एकतां identity जगुः ... objects of enjoy-

इतर जीवयोः with the two other Jivas.

XXXVI

What is the nature of Jiva and what is, again, the nature of the universe? The answer is thus stated :—

जीवो धीस्थचिदाभासो भवेद्भोक्ता हि कर्मकृत् ।
भोग्यरूपमिदं सर्वं जगत्स्याद्भूतभौतिकम् ॥ ३६ ॥

धीस्थः located in Buddhi (mind) चिदाभासः fallacious presentation of Consciousness कर्मकृत् the performer of activities भोक्ता (च) (as well as) the enjoyer हि because (तस्मात् therefore) जीवः भवेत् becomes Jiva भूतभौतिकं consisting of elements (भूतं) and their products (भौतिकं) भोग्यरूपं of the nature of the objects of enjoyment इदं सर्वं all this, जगत् universe स्यात् is called.

36. It is because the fallacious presentation of Consciousness (चिदाभासः) located in the Buddhi performs various[1] actions and enjoys[2] their results, therefore it is called Jiva. And all this, consisting of the elements[3] and their products[4] which are of the nature of the objects of enjoyment, is called Jagat (universe).

[1] *Various actions*—Such as cultivation, trade, sacrifice, worship, study of the Vedas, spiritual practices etc.

[2] *Enjoys*—Either in this world or in heaven.

[3] *Elements*—Ether, air, fire, water and earth.

[4] *Products*—Various animate and inanimate objects.

XXXVII

Both Jiva and Jagat are the products of Māyā; hence they are cognized so long as a man is in a state of ignorance.

अनादिकालमारभ्य मोक्षात्पूर्वमिदं द्वयम् ।
व्यवहारे स्थितं तस्मादुभयं व्यावहारिकम् ॥ ३७ ॥

इदं द्वयं these two मोक्षात्पूर्वं till one attains liberation अनादिकालमारभ्य from time without beginning व्यवहारे स्थितं have only empirical existence तस्मात् therefore उभयं both व्यावहारिकं (are) empirical (in nature).

37. These[1] two, dating from time without[2] beginning, have (only) empirical[3] existence and exist till[4] one attains liberation. Therefore both are called empirical.[5]

[1] *These two*—The Jiva and Jagat.

[2] *Without etc.*—The origin of Māyā which produces the conceptions of time, space and causation cannot be proved from the relative or the empirical standpoint. It is because we are in Māyā that we cannot know the cause of Māyā. Compare—

"प्रकृतिं पुरुषं चैव विद्ध्यनादी उभावपि" (गीता, १३-१९)

"Know both Prakriti and Purusha to be without beginning."

[3] *Empirical*—In the state of ignorance the ideas of knower, knowledge and known are possible and the existence of the universe as well as various activities connected with it are possible only through these concepts.

[4] *Till one etc.*—The world disappears when one attains liberation or Jnānam. Compare—

"गताः कलाः पंचदशप्रतिष्ठा देवाश्च सर्वे प्रतिदेवतासु ।
कर्माणि विज्ञानमयश्च आत्मा परेऽव्यये सर्वं एकी भवंति ॥
(मुं. उ. ३-२-७)

"Their fifteen parts enter into their elements, their Devas (the senses) into their (corresponding) Devas. Their deeds and their Self with all his knowledge become all one in the Highest Imperishable."

[5] *Empirical*—The Jiva and Jagat are neither real (पारमार्थिक) nor illusory (प्रातिभासिक). They are empirical or phenomenal (व्यावहारिक).

XXXVIII

The following doubt arises: if the individual self, as well as the cognized universe, existing from time immemorial, should last till one attains liberation, how is it possible to explain the scriptural passages dealing with creation, preservation and destruction and also waking, dream and deep sleep states? It is thus explained:—

चिदाभासस्थिता निद्रा विक्षेपावृतिरूपिणी ।
आवृत्य जीवजगती पूर्वे नूत्ने तु कल्पयेत् ॥ ३८ ॥

चिदाभासस्थिता located in (associated with) Consciousness as wrongly presented विक्षेपावृति-रूपिणी of the nature of projection and concealment निद्रा sleep पूर्वे at first जीवजगती the (individual) self and the cognized universe आवृत्य covering नूत्ने new तु but कल्पयेत् imagines.

38. Sleep, said to be associated with Consciousness wrongly presented (in the mind) and of the nature of concealment and projection, at first covers the (empirical) individual[1] self and the cognized universe, but[2] then imagines them (in dream) afresh.[3]

[1] *Individual etc.*—The individual self and the universe whose existence is perceived in the waking state.

[2] *But*—This is to show the distinction between the Jiva and Jagat perceived in the waking state (Vyāvahārika) and those of the dream state (Prātibhāsika).

[3] *Afresh*—That is, the Jiva and the Jagat cognized in dream which are apparently different from those of the waking state.

One of the scholiasts explains the Sloka in the following way :—

Nidrā means *Avidyā*, that is, a state in which the nature of reality is not known. This *Nidrā* or *Avidyā* merges (आवृत्य—प्रविलाप्य) everything within it at the time of deep sleep or cosmic dissolution ; Jiva, again, imagines them afresh at the time of waking. The word "imagines" means that they again become objects of experience. Jiva or the Chidābhāsa being itself a creation of Avidyā cannot properly be said to be the ground (आश्रय) of Avidyā. But from common experience, "I am ignorant" (अहं अज्ञः), such expression may be used.

It is on account of the belief in causality that the mind sees a causal relation between the experiences of the waking and the dream states.

XXXIX

Why are the Jiva and the Jagat, as cognized in dream, imaginary or illusory?

प्रतीतिकाल एवैते स्थितत्वात्प्रातिभासिके ।
न हि स्वप्नप्रबुद्धस्य पुनस्स्वप्ने स्थितिस्तयोः ॥ ३९ ॥

एते these two प्रतीतिकाले एव स्थितत्वात् on account of their having existed only during the period of (dream) experience प्रातिभासिके illusory (उच्यते are called) हि because स्वप्नप्रबुद्धस्य for one who has woke up from sleep स्वप्ने in (new) dream तयोः of those (Jiva and Jagat) पुनः again स्थितिः existence न not (seen).

39. These two objects (namely, the perceiving self and the perceived world) are illusory on account of their having existed only[1] during the period of (dream) experience. It is because no one after waking up from dream sees those objects when one dreams again.

[1] *Only*—These objects do not exist during the subsequent waking or dream states.

From this analogy it can be said that the entire world of experiences, perceived as real during the state of ignorance, are illusory or imaginary on account of their non-perception after the attainment of Knowledge.

XL

The following three stanzas point out the difference between the Jivas as conceived from the three standpoints stated above:—

प्रातिभासिकजीवो यस्तज्जगत्प्रातिभासिकम् ।
वास्तवं मन्यतेऽन्यस्तु मिथ्येति व्यावहारिकः ॥ ४० ॥

यः who (is) प्रातिभासिकः illusory (that is perceived in dream) जीवः Jiva (सः he) तत् that प्रातिभासिकं illusory (perceived in dream) जगत् world वास्तवं real मन्यते thinks तु but अन्यः other व्यावहारिकः empirical जीवः Jiva (तत् that) मिथ्या इति unreal (मन्यते thinks).

40. He who is the illusory[1] Jiva thinks the illusory world[2] as real[3] but the empirical[4] Jiva thinks (that world) as unreal[5].

[1] *Illusory*—Imagined in dream.

[2] *World*—The world that is perceived in dream.

[3] *Real*—Because such world exists as long as the dream Jiva exists in dream.

[4] *Empirical*—Vyāvahārika Jiva is he who considers himself to be the enjoyer etc., in the waking state. This Jiva is the reflection of Consciousness in the Buddhi.

[5] *Unreal*—To the Jiva of the waking state the entire dream-perceived world of subject and object appears as unreal.

The dream and the waking experiences, on account of their mutual contradictions, cannot be said to be real.

XLI

Now is described the nature of experiences of the Pāramārthika (Real) Jiva:—

व्यावहारिकजीवो यस्तज्जगद्व्यावहारिकम् ।
सत्यं प्रत्येति मिथ्येति मन्यते पारमार्थिकः ॥ ४१ ॥

यः who (is) व्यावहारिकः empirical जीवः Jiva सः he तत् that व्यावहारिकं empirical जगत् world सत्यं real प्रत्येति sees पारमार्थिकः the real (Jiva) (तत् that) मिथ्या इति unreal मन्यते thinks.

41. He who is the empirical[1] Jiva sees this empirical[2] world as real.[3] But the real[4] Jiva knows it[5] to be unreal.

[1] *Empirical*—See *ante.* sloka 36.

[2] *Empirical*—The world of waking experiences created by Māyā.

[3] *Real*—As existing in past, present and future. It is because the relative world exists as long as the Jiva, its perceiver, exists.

[4] *Real Jiva*—The Jiva that is the witness of the three states.

[5] *It*—The world and its experiences in the waking state.

[6] *Unreal*—Because such world and its experiences are not perceived in deep sleep.

XLII

The Pāramārthika Jiva as distinguished from the Jivas of the waking and dream experiences is identical with Brahman.

पारमार्थिकजीवस्तु ब्रह्मैक्यं पारमार्थिकम् ।
प्रत्येति वीक्षते नान्यद्वीक्षते त्वनृतात्मना ॥ ४२ ॥

पारमार्थिकजीवः the real Jiva तु but ब्रह्मैक्यं identity with Brahman पारमार्थिकं real प्रत्येति knows

अन्यत् other न वीक्षते does not see अनृतात्मना as unreal तु but वीक्षते sees.

42. But the Pāramārthika Jiva knows its identity with Brahman to be (alone) real. He does not see the other,[1] (if he sees the other) he knows it to be illusory.[2]

[1] *Other*—He does not see any existence other than Brahman. Comp. "यत्र नान्यत्पश्यति" (छां. उ. ७-२४-१) "where one does not see the other". "यत्र त्वस्य सर्वमात्मैवा भूत्" (बृ. उ. २-४-१४) "when the Self is only all this"

[2] *Illusory*—If the Pāramārthika Jiva comes back to the relative plane of Consciousness he knows the world and the reflected Consciousness (Jiva) to be unreal.

The Jiva so long as it does not know the distinction between the Witness (दृक्) and the perceived world (दृश्य) thinks the aggregate of body, mind, sense-organ etc., as the seer and the object (perceived world) as real. The Vyāvahārika Jiva is he who knows the ego (seer) as distinct from the aggregate of the mind, body and sense-organ etc., and thinks of the world not as real but the creation of the causal Self ultimately disappearing in it. He further knows this causal Self (Saguna Brahman) alone to be real. But the Pāramārthika Jiva knows this causal relation to be unreal. The Brahman does not produce or manifest the world of ego and non-ego. The idea of Jiva is due to a false superimposition upon Brahman. It is like the superimposition of the snake-idea on the rope.

XLIII–XLIV

The following doubt arises:—The Jivas known as Vyāvahārika (experiencer of the waking state) and Prātibhāsika (experiencer of the dream state) on account of their being products of Avidyā, are insentient by nature. Then how can they be described as Jiva? For Jiva is the same as the Jivātma as the Sruti says, "Entering by this *living self*" (*Chand. Up.* 6-3-2, 3). The Brahman itself has entered into the *Devatā* (shining element), of the nature of fire, earth, water, in the form of a *Jivātma* and manifested different names and forms. The doubt is thus solved :—

माधुर्यद्रवशैत्यानि नीरधर्मास्तरङ्गके ।

अनुगम्याथ तन्निष्ठे फेनेऽप्यनुगता यथा ॥ ४३ ॥

साक्षिस्थास्सच्चिदानन्दास्सम्बंधाद्व्यावहारिके ।

तद्द्वारेणानुगच्छंति तथैव प्रातिभासिके ॥ ४४ ॥

माधुर्यद्रवशैत्यानि sweetness, fluidity and coldness, नीरधर्माः characteristics of water तरंगके in the wave अनुगम्य inhering तन्निष्ठे फेने in the foam of which it (wave) is the substratum अपि also यथा अनुगता as inheres साक्षिस्थाः the inherent characteristics of Sākshin सच्चिदानन्दाः Existence, Consciousness and Bliss संबन्धात् on account of relation व्यावहारिके in the Vyāvahārika Jiva अनुगच्छन्ति inhere तद्द्वारेण through it प्रातिभासिके in the Prātibhāsika Jiva तथैव similarly (अनुगच्छन्ति inhere).

43-44. As such characteristics of water as sweetness, fluidity and coldness appear to inhere in the waves,[1] and then also in the foams of which the waves are the substratum, so also Existence,[2] Consciousness and Bliss which are the (natural characteristics of Sākshin) appear to[3] inhere in the Vyāvahārika Jiva[4] on account of its relation[5] (with Sākshin) and through it similarly inhere in the Prātibhāsika[6] Jiva.

[1] *Waves*—The substratum of waves is water. The characteristics of the substratum appear to inhere in that which is substrated. The water appears as waves and the waves as foams. There is no difference between them except in respect of names and forms. Again, the foams, waves and water cannot be separated from sweetness, fluidity and coldness The substance is, according to Vedānta, the same as the quality.

[2] *Existence etc.*—These are the natural characteristics (स्वरूपलक्षण) of Sākshin or Brahman. As a matter of fact, Sākshin is identical with Satchidānanda.

[3] *To inhere in*—It is because the Vyāvahārika Jiva, including the perceived universe, is the illusory appearance (Ārōpita) falsely superimposed upon Brahman. Therefore the characteristics of Brahman appear to inhere in the Jiva and the Jagat.

[4] *Jiva*—Both the Vyāvahārika Jiva and the Prātibhāsika Jiva include the worlds or the non-egos perceived in the waking and dream states.

[5] *Relation*—This relation is seen from the causal or relative standpoint. From the standpoint of Brahman there is no Jiva, Vyāvahārika or Prātibhāsika and hence no relation.

[6] *Prātibhāsika Jiva*—Both the ego and the non-ego cognized in dream also have the characteristics of Existence, Consciousness and Bliss.

XLV

This is how the characteristics of Ātman are superimposed (अध्यारोप) upon the seer and the seen. Now comes the negation (अपवाद) of this erroneous superimposition.

लये फेनस्य तद्धर्मा द्रवाद्यास्स्युस्तरङ्गके ।
तस्यापि विलये नीरे तिष्ठंत्येते यथा पुरा ॥ ४५ ॥

फेनस्य लये with the disappearance of the foam तद्धर्माः its characteristics द्रवाद्याः such as fluidity etc. तरङ्गके in the wave स्युः exist तस्यापि विलये with its disappearance again एते these यथा पुरा as before नीरे in the water तिष्ठन्ति exist.

45. With the disappearance of the foam[1] (in the wave), its characteristics such as fluidity etc. merge in the wave; again with the disappearance of the wave[2] in the water, these characteristics merge, as[3] before, in the water.

[1] *Foam*—This is an appearance. The wave appears as the foam.

[2] *Wave*—This is also an appearance of water, which is the ultimate substratum.

[3] *As before*—Fluidity, coldness and sweetness were what constituted water before waves and foams appeared. Now after the disappearance of wave and foam in the water, these characteristics are also found to exist in their antecedent forms, as water from which they cannot be separated. Water always exists. Foams etc. have no existence separate from water. They appear from and disappear in water. They are nothing but water in another form.

XLVI

Now the meaning that we get from the illustration is applied to the object illustrated :—

प्रातिभासिकजीवस्य लये स्युर्व्यावहारिके ।
तल्लये सच्चिदानंदाः पर्यवस्यंति साक्षिणि ॥ ४६ ॥

प्रातिभासिकस्य जीवस्य लये with the disappearance of the Prātibhāsika Jiva (सच्चिदानन्दाः the characteristics of Existence, Consciousness and Bliss) व्यावहारिके in the Vyāvahārika (empirical) Jiva स्युः exist तल्लये with the disappearance of that सच्चिदानन्दाः characteristics of Existence, Consciousness and Bliss साक्षिणि in Sākshin पर्यवस्यान्ति merge.

46. With the disappearance of the Prātibhāsika[1] Jiva (in the Vyāvahārika Jiva) Existence, Consciousness and Bliss (which are its characteristics) merge in the Vyāvahārika Jiva. When that also disappears (in Sākshin) these characteristics (finally) merge in Sākshin.[2]

[1] *Prātibhāsika Jiva*—This and the Vyāvahārika Jiva include the worlds perceived by them respectively.

[2] *Sākshin*—That is, Brahman which is identical with Self. Existence, Consciousness and Bliss which are imagined to be qualities of Brahman are, in reality, the same as Brahman.

As with the merging of foam, wave etc. in the water, their fluidity etc. disappear therein, even so with the mergence of the Prātibhāṣika Jiva and the Vyāvahārika Jiva in Sākshin (that is, in Brahman at the time of deep sleep and Mukti respectively) the characteristics, such as Existence etc. inhering in them, disappear in Brahman. For names and forms as well as the characteristics belonging to them have no other existence apart from Brahman. They appear out of and disappear in Brahman—Brahman or Sākshin. Its existence cannot be denied, in the past, the present or the future nor in the states of waking, dream or deep sleep. The Vyāvahārika Jiva and the world that it perceives are non-existent before creation and after dissolution. They exist only during the period of ignorance. They appear out of Brahman, inhere in Brahman and finally disappear in Brahman. As foam and wave have no existence apart from water, so also the entire universe consisting of the ego and the non-ego have no existence apart from Brahman. Verily all that exists *is* Brahman.

Printed in the USA
CPSIA information can be obtained
at www.ICGtesting.com
LVHW070241080524
779424LV00002B/454